FRECKLES!

BY: DA BUTLER

Dedicated to all of our beautiful,
freckled friends and family!

Freckles on my face, what a
beautiful sight to see.
I love my little freckles
because they show the real me.

What makes you different, your
skin, your hair, your eyes?
Each of us a present
made of our own surprise.

Everyone is different
their own unique way.
Freckles make me happy I
can talk of them all day.

My face is full of freckles from
my cheeks to the tip of my nose.
As I get a little older my
freckles too will grow!

The sunshine makes me happy,
my freckles come to view.
Let me look at you close up
maybe you have freckles too!

Freckles on my face, what a
beautiful sight to see.
I love my little freckles,
come and see the real me!